READY...SET...NAP!

A No-Nonsense Guide to Get Your Toddler to Nap in a Weekend

SANDRA SIKONIA

READY, SET, NAP! A NO-NONSENSE GUIDE TO GET YOUR TODDLER TO NAP IN A WEEKEND.

TABLE of CONTENTS

INTRODUCTION

I AM A MOM, and I have fucked up *a lot*. One thing I really fucked up was getting my first kid to properly take a nap. For years, my husband and I struggled with naptime for our daughter. No matter what we tried, she refused to nap for us in her own bed at naptime. However, this fucking up led to the need to fix the situation. Once I woke up to what was going on, I was able to remedy this problem and get my child napping. To learn how I accomplished this feat, read on.

I developed this technique, tweaked and perfected it, when my child was already a toddler. We had suffered years of unconventional naptimes or no napping at all, and the techniques described here ended our frustration in just one weekend! This book is the information I wish I was able to give to my past-self, which would have saved me years of turmoil over napping. I hope that my message to my "pre-nap" self can help others in the same difficult situation.

If you're a parent or guardian to a child who won't nap conventionally, the information in this book is for you. This guide provides easy-to-follow steps that can be implemented in only one weekend.

2

The TIWIKEs
Things I Wish I Knew Earlier

AS A FIRST TIME parent, there was a lot about children I never knew, and plenty of things I learned along the way that I wish I could send back in time to my old self. These are the three most important things I wish I knew earlier, which become crucial for attempts at naptime regulation.

TIWIKE #1: Babies/Kids have major FOMO (Fear Of Missing Out)

Seriously, most kids would never eat, nap or do so many other essential things if we didn't force them. They don't want to miss out and are having fun living life and loving it. FOMO can make many children dread and resist naptime.

When my child was a toddler, she refused to nap because she was afraid of missing out on what we were doing during the day. Nothing could convince her she wouldn't miss out on life, and when we'd put her down for naptime, she'd refuse to stay in bed, always staying awake so she could see and be near to us. FOMO is a serious detractor from napping.

TIWIKE #2: Babies/Kids are master manipulators

Not joking here. These little guys know what they are doing! They know how to distract and stall, and they do whatever they can to get what they want. If your child doesn't want to nap, chances are he or she will try many different tactics to avoid the dreaded activity.

My child hated conventional naptime but didn't mind

sleeping in her stroller or in the car. For years she manipulated us into allowing her to have naptime her way, instead of our way. It is hard looking back, seeing how our baby and, later, toddler was able to manipulate us to avoid napping the way we wanted her to nap.

TIWIKE #3: Babies/Kids cry

Legitimately, I didn't understand this as a first-time mom. I knew that babies cried when something was wrong, like when they were hungry, had a dirty diaper, etc., but I didn't realize that they also could cry when all their important needs were met. For example, they often use crying as part of a plan related to TIWIKE #2.

When it was time for napping, our child often threw tantrums, crying loudly to end the naptime. Like many parents struggling with their child's naps, the crying was such a good manipulation, we'd allow her to come out of her room. If only we had known what we know now, we wouldn't have allowed her crying and manipulations to stop her from having productive and traditional naptimes.

I think it's clear from the information above that I had next-to-no knowledge of babies or children prior to having children of my own. You may be thinking, "Should I take advice from someone who doesn't have a PhD related to children?" Well, Dr. PhD likely has less experience with a crappy napper, because he never would have ended up in this position. My ability to truly identify with how one ends up here, as well as my firsthand knowledge of how to stop the madness, gives me the upper hand on Dr. PhD when it comes to naptime.

After I used the techniques described in this guide, my toddler finally napped conventionally. Years of struggling with my child led me to develop this approach. Frustrated with my child's naptime disasters, I looked to books for guidance, but the advice didn't seem right. Either the authors wanted a stricter schedule than my life permitted, or the techniques simply didn't work. Most of the time it seemed like the advice was meant to guide a person who was preparing ahead of time and learning how to get a child to sleep well from the start as opposed to someone in the middle of a full-blown nap disaster.

Desperate for an answer to my problems, I decided to come up with my own method. After observing positive reinforcement being used successfully at my child's daycare, and stewing over the advice books I'd read, I came up with the technique described in this guide. With this method my child went from being a terrible napper who would cry and throw fits, manipulating my husband and me every naptime, to a successful napper in only one weekend. Now, with this helpful guide, your child can become a napper too!

3
BACKSTORY

THIS LEADS ME TO how I messed up naptime and learned how to fix it. My story may ring true for you too, and if so, will help you with step one in "Before Starting."

Our first kid was a real firecracker from day one, and my husband and I thought she was "really special." Of course, she *is* really special, but we thought that standard procedures didn't apply to us and "just didn't work" for *our* kid.

When anyone gave us advice on parenting, like for her not napping conventionally, we would say and think, "But no, you don't understand. She *is* different. She just won't do it. She won't slow down. She just cries and cries if we try (TIWIKE #2 and #3 in action). We have to take her on a walk or drive, and trick her into falling asleep (which she did beautifully)."

I was home with her until she was seven-months-old. I walked with her or drove her in the car every time she needed a nap, and typically stayed walking or driving the whole time. On top of that, other people close to us who watched her, like her grandparents, had to do this same thing. If they didn't or they couldn't for some reason, she turned into a nightmare, especially as she got older. Eventually, it was embarrassing to get a babysitter, which we rarely did. But when we did, we would just say, "She doesn't really nap," and know that we would come home to a mess and have to take her on a "nap walk" (we did them so often we called them this). Ugh. I feel your frustration if this is where you are right now.

I remember thinking, "How will she ever go to daycare?

Will they kick her out since she can't nap?"

She did go to daycare, and guess what? She napped. Did this convince us she could nap? Nope.

Looking back, it is hard to understand how that didn't convince us. I told myself that she must be only able to nap there because of the influence of other babies napping. So, because we didn't believe she could nap at home, and when we occasionally "tried" to get her to nap at home, she wouldn't, we continued with the good ol' standby, the "nap walk."

I remember telling people, "She naps at school but just won't at home," and, "She sleeps well at night and just doesn't nap well."

The common theme here is she napped or slept well when she *had* to. The people at the daycare weren't going to take our "special" baby (eventually toddler) on a "nap walk." They had other babies to take care of. So, they figured it out. They were committed because they had to be.

Similarly, she slept well at night because, while we did employ the "nap walk" on a few evenings, we were far more committed to getting her to sleep in the evening for many reasons. Most of the time we were tired as shit and sometimes it was cold. We didn't want to go outside in the dark of night ourselves, let alone with our baby. Also, walking with a stroller in the house was hard, weird, and it marked up the baseboards and door frames. We actually did do these indoor "nap walks" at night on occasion, but they seemed less sustainable than daytime "nap walks."

So, because we were committed to making sleeping at night happen, it happened. Eventually. It could have happened faster if I knew TIWIKE #3. I remember thinking, "It will get better when she is older." It didn't get better. In fact, we were just getting deeper and deeper.

Our daughter started not liking the stroller so we were limited to "nap drives." I justified these by changing our daily schedule such that we did out-of-the-house errands when she was sleeping. I said, trying to convince myself this was reasonable, "I don't want to be tied down to a nap schedule so I can't go out and do anything. The fact that she naps in the car allows us to do more." Ugh. Nope.

Most of the time my husband and I would go out together and, after driving until she fell asleep, one of us would stay in the car while the other grocery shopped or went to the hardware store, or whatever needed doing. Sometimes one of us would take her out on a drive while the other did things at home. Regardless, sometimes this "worked out" but we spent *a lot* of time sitting in the car waiting for her to wake up. As she became a toddler, sometimes it would take a long time for her to fall asleep, so we would spend up to an hour getting her to fall asleep and then the length of her nap after that in the car!

I remember thinking, "Well, we are in so deep in this nap disaster, there is no getting out. Can I make it, doing this, until she doesn't need to nap anymore?" I literally was Googling, "At what age do kids stop taking naps?" and doing the math to see if I could stomach it for that many more *years.*

Finally, one day, after contemplating this question again, I said, "NO! I cannot make it! This is <u>over.</u>"

While your napping mess might not be identical to what I have described, if you are in a situation like this where your kid "won't nap," there is still hope. Many children display wild behaviors to escape naptime, to the dismay of parents like me and my husband. After deciding not to settle for my toddler's naptime struggle, I tried different techniques to resolve the issue. Then, I developed the methods described here, and all of our lives, ours and our child's, changed for the better.

4

BEFORE STARTING

1. *REALIZE YOUR KID* *can nap and you are letting this no-napping thing continue.*

This is <u>**HUGE**</u>. I cannot emphasize this enough. If you cannot acknowledge this, then I am sorry to say, you are likely to continue whatever napping nightmare is going on. You must recognize that you have allowed this situation to get to this point. I understand this can be hard because we are all just out here surviving. We are doing our best. But, while we are doing our best, we can fuck up. I fucked up and you fucked up, but I got out and so can you. You can get out of this situation and make your life, and your kid's life, better. Everyone is better with better sleep.

If you are struggling with this, I ask you to consider the following.

Even if your kid isn't in daycare, try to ask yourself, *if* you were to have a professional care for your child, either in home or at a daycare, would the professional be doing what you are doing to get your kid to sleep?

Would they be squeezing in with them on a recliner in the playroom, trapped and unable to move for hours? Would they be loading them into the car and driving around for hours, or whatever you are doing, because your kid will "only nap like that"?

NO! They would get your kid to nap conventionally, because they wouldn't spend their days like that.

You might be saying, as I once did, "Well, they are professionals and I am not and I don't know what to do!"

I was like you too. By insisting that my child was special and that I wasn't a professional, I allowed the problem to magnify. It was only after I hit rock bottom, after years of allowing my "special" child to get away with nap drives and tantrums, that I had the courage to say enough was enough and began attempts at remedying the problem of naptime. It was like a lightbulb going off. I, and I alone, had the power to change my situation with my toddler. I would not revert back to car naps and other tactics that "worked." I would emerge triumphantly from my efforts with a child who napped well.

There wasn't a guidebook for me at the time. I had to get so low, I was contemplating the situation dragging on for years, until my child no longer needed napping. Now, with this book, you can learn from my mistakes and successes. Accepting responsibility for your child's behavior is only the first step, but an important one. Once you've accomplished this, you'll be ready to conquer the next steps.

2. MENTALLY PREPARE YOURSELF.

You must be all-in on this. There is no, "I will try this method out and see if it works." That kind of attitude will get you nowhere and is what you have already been doing.

You have likely been occasionally "trying" to get your kid to nap conventionally when you really don't feel like doing whatever it is you have been doing to get your kid to nap. You likely try really hard to get your kid to nap, before you finally give up and feel super frustrated.

Attitudes to Have	Attitudes Not to Have
✓ This is happening	✗ I am not sure I can do this
✓ I am doing this	✗ I will try
✓ My kid can nap	✗ My kid just really needs ____ to nap
✓ I am done letting this continue	✗ I am going to do whatever to survive the day
✓ I will never do ______ to let my kid nap again	✗ It's not that long until they won't need a nap anymore, right?

For this method to work, you must be ready to say "Never again. Seriously. Never again will I do ______ (fill in the blank with whatever craziness you have been doing to get your kid to sleep)."

This plan does not take a lot of time, but it does take you being confident that weird naps are over and your kid <u>will</u> nap conventionally. This is absolutely essential.

3. PREPARE THE SPACE.

You will need to have a couple items prepared ahead of getting your kid to nap.

- A darkened room.

The room must be able to get quite dark. I highly recommend room blackout shades or curtains, but do whatever you have to do. If that means taping loads of black construction paper to the window, do that. If it means buying some fancy room darkening window coverings, do that. But whatever you do, make sure the room gets dark. This helps set the mood as well as avoid issues with TIWIKE #1. To your toddler, it will feel less like there is anything to miss out on if it is dark.

- A way to play a story.

When it comes time to actually take the nap, even when you have done all the prep work discussed here, your kid will employ TIWIKE #2 tactics. You are going to have to fend them off by saying, "no" to them, but you want to have something to offer. That something is playing them a story. This way you can say kindly, "No, I am not going to read you a story, but I can play you a story after you are lying down."

The story allows the caregiver to separate from the child, and cuts off immediate and easy access to more TIWIKE tactics from the child. Having a story played by a neutral device, rather than being read by a parent in the room, keeps the space free from distraction. If a caregiver was to stay in the room and read, the child would likely continue to use TIWIKE tactics and be less likely to fall asleep. Also, a story time device doesn't need the extra reading lamp or other distracting objects required by a reader.

There are a number of ways to play a story. You can play a story from your phone or tablet directly, connect wirelessly to a speaker, or some kids' clocks have the capability to play a story. When selecting a method, know that you cannot be in the room during naptime. If you choose to play directly from a phone or tablet, the story must be playing in the background with the screen off to keep the room dark and calm. However you play a story, it should be a pre-sleeping story that is calming and soothing both in story and in sound.

- Treats

You will be rewarding your child for when they take a nap. You also want to be able to tell your child what the reward will be to increase their interest in taking said nap. I suggest offering two gummy bears. Two is a good amount because it is not just one, but it isn't a bunch either. Also, gummy bears are a good treat because they take a little while for the kids to eat and they aren't messy. You can choose whatever reward you want, but I am going to *highly recommend* it be candy, and that it is something you are comfortable giving your kid after each nap. Ask yourself, could I give two gummy bears, two M&Ms or the like to my kid once a day for a while to get them to nap properly and stop the madness? I bet the answer is yes.

Make sure you have your blackout shades installed, understand and have practiced using your story playing device, and have treats on hand but tucked out of sight of your child. Keeping them stashed away is important because you don't want them to be a distraction. You do, however, want to be able to grab them right after nap time to give to your child. They only need to see the two treats when a nap is over and do not need to see the container. You also don't want to be fumbling with your new shades, or confused on how to get the story to play when it is naptime.

4. PLAN THE TIME.

You will need to find two days that you can dedicate to napping. It does not mean you can't do other things on these days, but it <u>really</u> limits what you can do and when you can do it, so for now, you can't have other plans.

Two days is the perfect amount of time to prove to yourself and your child that a normal naptime routine can be achieved. It's long enough to show your toddler or child how serious you are, and also enough time to establish a preliminary set of rules to follow. Once you know naptime works with the methods employed, you can feel confident utilizing these steps for a formal naptime.

To make this a little easier, let's say that you are choosing to do this on a weekend (even though you can do it any two days in a row if that is available to you). You will need to ensure that you have two days that are free of requirements of any kind, and that you can focus on fixing this. It can be hard to give up a weekend, but just imagine what you will be gaining when you get your kid to nap. No more insane grouchiness. No more whatever crazy thing you are currently doing to get your kid to sleep. No more feeling guilty or ashamed of your child's napping situation.

5. PREPARE YOUR CHILD

Now that you have checked off steps 1-4, you are ready to prepare your kid. Let your kid know what is going to happen. It will sound something like this, "Hey, buddy, this weekend you are going to take a nap in your bed/crib and after you nap you are going to get two gummy bears. Cool!" Keep the conversation light and exciting, but also to the point. This is NOT a question. This is a STATEMENT of what WILL happen. It is very important that you use statements and not questions. You will want to keep repeating this multiple times a day in the few days prior to the official start of nap days. You can mix up what you say but keep it light, positive and to the point.

Below are some examples of things you might say to mix it up and keep reminding your child of what is going to happen.	All of the below items or anything like it are no-gos for talking about the start of napping.
✔ Remember that on Saturday, you are going to take a nap in your bed/crib and after you will get two gummy bears.	✘ Are you going to take a nap on Saturday?
✔ What do you get after you take your nap on Saturday? Right! Two gummy bears.	✘ Doesn't it sound great to take a nap in your bed/crib on Saturday?
✔ On Saturday you are going to take a nap like you do at daycare and after your nap you are going to get two gummy bears.	✘ Are you excited to take a nap in your bed/crib on Saturday?
✔ Grandma is going to be so proud of you after you take your nap on Saturday. Remember that after your nap you get two gummy bears.	
✔ Ms. Allison is going to be so proud of you when you take your nap on Saturday. Oh, yeah, and remember — you are going to get two gummy bears after you take your nap.	

6. *GETTING TO IT*

Once you have found a weekend that works for you, and it is blocked off from other responsibilities, you should be aware of what you can and cannot do on these days. You can take your kid out, pre-nap, close to your home. In fact, I recommend that you take your child out and do some activity to ensure they are tired and ready to nap when it is time. You can, for example, take your kid to the park near your home in the morning, or on a morning walk in your neighborhood, or to get breakfast near where you live, or to an indoor playground near your house. The pre-nap activities must be *near your home (I mean really near your home — no more than a 5-7 minute drive or walk).*

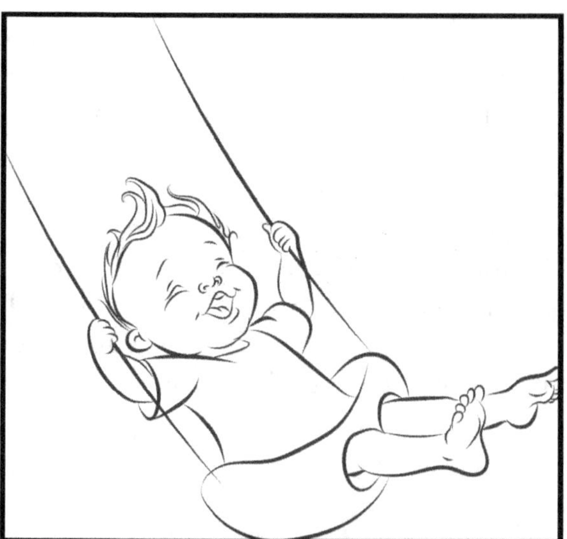

The pre-nap activities are good because a.) it is nice to get out and do something for both you and your kid, and b.) it can help your child be more prepared for napping if they have gotten out and done something. It is essential that the activities are close to your home because you cannot have your child fall asleep in the car or stroller returning from the activity. It is extremely important that they have not napped, even for a minute. If they are really worn out from the pre-nap activity, you must keep them awake for the short (because it is really close, right?) drive or walk home. If this means singing to them, talking to them or touching their leg or arm, do it. If they fall asleep, you cannot continue, but I know you won't let that happen because you are all-in on fixing this napping mess.

You already know when your kid naps because you have been doing whatever with them already to get them to nap. So, if you usually start packing them into the stroller at 12:30, then that is when they nap. If you start cuddling up to them in the recliner at 1pm, then that is when they nap. Make sure your activity is pre-nap time and…? That's right, "close to home."

Remind your child many times the first day about their nap. "Remember, after we go to the park, we are going to come back and you are going to take a nap in your bed." "When we get home, it is going to be time for a nap and after your nap you get two treats."

If at all possible, your child can have a snack/lunch while you are out on the pre-nap activity, so there is one less activity for them to use with TIWIKE #2. Additionally, these days are days to limit fluid intake, as "needing to go to the bathroom" is more TIWIKE #2 ammunition.

5

READY...SET...NAP!

7. *IT'S GAME TIME.*

After your pre-nap activity, immediately begin preparing your child for napping. Remind your child that it is time to take a nap and walk with them directly to their bed/crib. At this time they are likely to start employing TIWIKE #2 techniques. Stay focused on the task at hand. They are napping. Period. End of story.

Here are examples of ways to help handle common TIWIKE #2 techniques.

TIWIKE #2 Technique	Response
I don't want to take a nap + crying	It is nap time and we are all taking a nap now.
I am hungry	We all just ate. Right now it is nap time. I can play you a story once you are lying down.
I need to go to the bathroom	We can go to the bathroom one time but we are coming right back here and taking a nap after we go potty. (Walk to restroom with them and walk them back after using the restroom)
I need to go to the bathroom again	We just went to the bathroom. It is nap time now. I am going to turn on the story and let you nap.
Gets out of bed and walks out	Bring child back to bed. Remind the child that it is nap time and that everyone is taking a nap now. If necessary, remind them that they will be taking a nap and no other activites will be happening until after napping.
Can you sleep in here with me?	No, I can't sleep in here with you but I can come check on you.
Can you read to me?	No, but I can turn on a story for you. (I get that we all want to say yes to reading and reading is great and all, we all get that, but this is not the time. This is just TIWIKE #2 in disguise).
Can you adjust the temperature, move something, turn something, get me something, etc?	No, I am going to let you take your nap. I will turn the story on for you.

Do's and Don'ts

Do	Don't
Do keep things matter of fact.	Don't discuss fun stuff you will do after nap.
Do stick to the plan no matter how long it takes to get them to nap.	Don't give up.
Do be firm.	Don't be aggressive.

It is possible that it may take many hours to get your child to nap and that is okay. This is unfamiliar to them and they are testing you to make sure your are serious (and you ARE).

It is important when the nap actually happens that it is long enough to make you feel confident your child actually fell asleep and wasn't just laying there. When he or she wakes up from the nap you want to be ready to grab the two treats and greet them.

Immediately say something inspiring like, "I am so proud of you for taking your nap. Here are your two treats. Great job." As they wake up and start moving again, continue offering praise and encouragement for a job well done. Everyone likes to hear they did a great job, even toddlers!

Examples of praise statements:

✔ I am so proud of you for taking a nap!

✔ That was so cool how you took a nap and then you got your two treats!

✔ Ms. Allison (teacher, grandparents, whoever) is going to be so proud of you that you took a nap in your bed!

After day one is complete, you can gear up to repeat it

on day two. Remember how it was possible that day one could take hours to get your kid to nap? It is also possible that day one will go very well, and day two will take hours. That is okay. The children are just testing to make sure you really plan to keep having them nap and seeing if they can TIWIKE #2 themselves out of it.

When day two arrives, start the process over. Prepare your kid: remind them that they will be taking a nap like they did the day before and they will get two treats again. Yay! Take them to do a pre-nap activity close to home, bring them home to nap, give them two treats and praise. DO NOT GIVE UP.

8. *AFTER THE WEEKEND*

Once you have two nap days under your belt, that hard work is over. Your kid knows you are serious about having them nap traditionally at home and they have two successful naps under their belt. Now, reinforcement is what is needed. It is important for at least six additional days, you keep to the same plan. This means for these six days, no going out of town and having the kids nap in the car, or heading out to run errands and having them nap in between. It is important they get a solid understanding that you are going to have them nap traditionally and the first two days weren't a fluke. After the six days, if you need or want to go out of town and need to have your kid nap in the car it is okay, just talk to them about it. Say, "Today we are going to go on a long car drive out of town, and so it is okay if you fall asleep in the car. When we are at home, we nap in our crib/bed, but because we will be driving during naptime today, it is okay if you sleep in the car."

You may be wondering how this works if you chose a weekend. Let's say for example you chose your two nap days to be on the weekend. Your nap days are complete, and your child goes to childcare during the week. There is no reason to be concerned that you won't be practicing and re-inforcing naptime rituals until the following weekend. First, they are probably napping at childcare as we discussed earlier. Kids are super good at adapting, which is why many kids, like mine, can nap at school but not at home. What is important is that the next weekend, when they are with you, you continue the process. You will need to continue the process for three additional weekends before adding any disruption, like out of town adventures, to ensure that the traditional nap is properly reinforced.

Do you have to give your kids two treats after napping forever? No, but I bet you would now that you know how great having a napper is, amiright? But seriously, you should continue to give them the two treats for the six additional days. After the six additional days, continue to give them two treats when they ask for them but don't offer. The asking should taper naturally but if not, once the nap is completely established and solidly reinforced, if needed, you can say something like, "You are a big kid and we don't get treats for naptime anymore, but we can have treats ______(you fill in the blank here — for special occasions, when we go to Grandma's house, at birthday parties, etc.)."

6

SUMMARY

PARENTING STRUGGLES AND mishaps happen. We are all capable of making mistakes and causing ourselves trouble. That was me with my first child. Now you have the opportunity to learn from my mistakes and triumphs, whether your child is a notorious naptime scoundrel or you're interested in what to do if your child becomes one.

Let's review the eight important steps to follow:

1. Understand what has led you to this situation and the part you've played in your child's behavior.
2. Mentally prepare yourself for change. Be ready to be firm and committed.
3. Prepare the space. Make sure the space you've chosen has what you need, such as no lighting, a comfortable and quiet sleeping area, a way to play a story, treats, etc..
4. Plan the time. You want to do this on a weekend or other open two-day stretch.
5. Prepare your child. Remember to be excited yet firm. Prime your child with clear statements like, "This weekend you'll be napping after the park, and then you can have two treats."
6. Getting to it. While your child has their pre-nap activity, gently remind them of the upcoming nap event.
7. It's game time. Prepare your child and set them down to nap. Use the tactics discussscd to power through any tough-napper backlash. Be gentle, but firm.

8.   After the weekend. Ensure your kid has the most chances of success by repeating these steps for at least six additional days. This builds a habit and reinforces proper behavior.

Congratulations, your child is officially a napper!

7

CONCLUSION

DON'T SETTLE FOR your child being unable to nap, or only being able to nap if other conditions are met. If you're like me, driving your child in a car or taking nap walks might seem like the only solution to nap time. Accept responsibility for your child being a poor napper and get started on the rest of your life. No more living around the demands of children who won't nap. Now, with this simple eight step guide, you can escape the nightmare of parenting a child who refuses traditional napping!

I developed this technique after countless books and the advice of family and friends were not providing what I needed to get out of my napping nightmare. Watching how my toddler was treated at daycare, I had a lightbulb moment. I needed to clean up my act as a mom when it came to nap time, so I pulled together my best understandings of material I read, saw, or heard and created this eight-step plan of action. The positive reinforcement and firm attitude are easy to incorporate into your life, and the change is well worth the effort. One weekend to learn the technique, then three more weekends practicing is something anyone can afford and is worth the effort when you know your child sleeps at nap time, without the fuss. I used these steps to transform my crappy napper and I'll never go back to the old habits of nap walks, tantrums, and missed nap times again! Use these eight steps to correct *your* child's nap time and get your life and sanity back for good!

www.ingramcontent.com/pod-product-compliance
Lightning Source LLC
Chambersburg PA
CBHW050710250726

48662CB00002B/953